THE LITTLE BOOK OF
LAKE DISTRICT FACTS

Wainwright started work on
the first page of his Pictorial
Guide to the Lakeland Fells
on 9 November 1952

The name Scafell Pike comes from Old Norse. Skalli Fijall (the fell with the bald summit)

There's only one
actual lake in
the Lake District

The Lake District is home to England's highest peak

Windermere
is home to
18 islands

The Lake District is one of the only places in the UK where you can see red squirrels

Beatrix Potter
the creator of
Peter Rabbit,
lived in Sawrey

The Lake District inspired famous poet William Wordsworth

Sticky Toffee Pudding
was Invented in
the Lake District

A quarter of the UK's
population visit each year

Romney's Kendal Mint Cake was invented by mistake, after the creator took his eye off the pan while making a batch of clear mints

Pencils were Invented
in the Lake District

The Lakes District
is home of the
Original Mass Protest

In 1810 William
Wordsworth published
"Guide to the Lakes"

In the year 1895 Lake
Windermere froze
for 6 weeks

The Lake District
has its own castle

There are six times
more sheep than people
in the Lake District

One of the lakes
is a tomb of
two villages

The Lake District
has its own
Stonehenge

Scafell Pike was formed 450 million years ago

The Lake District
is home to the deepest
bodies of Water and
the Highest Peaks

In a Pub in
Santon Bridge you can
try to become the
"World's Biggest Liar"

Whitehaven was once
invaded by Americans,
who got distracted
by the local ale

Beatrix Potter, creator
of Peter Rabbit, was
an award-winning
cumbrian sheep farmer

The Lake District
National Park covers
2,292 square kilometres
(or 885 square miles)

In 2017 there was a 6.6% increase in the numbers of visitors staying in non-serviced accommodation on the previous year

Mountains in the Lake District are actually older than the Himalayas, which are only about 50 million years old

Just over 40,000 people live in the Lake District National Park

In 1930 Henry Segrave took to Lake Windermere to break the world water speed record aboard Miss England II

At the 10th annual stone skimming event, Alex Lewis broke the current record by an amazing 7 metres

Windermere and Bowness were the second part of England to have electric street lighting, which was supplied by a hydro-electric plant at Troutbeck Bridge

Blencathra is 868 m/2,848ft above sea level, making it the 14th highest Lake District peak

The area was designated
a national park
on 9 May 1951

The Vendace (Coregonus Vandesius) is England's rarest species of fish, and is found only in the Lake District.

The National Park
includes 26 miles of
coastline and estuaries

"Winder" is a derivative of the Norse name Vinandr. While "mere" is an old English word for a body of water

There are four Michelin-Starred Restaurants in the Lake District

Keswick became widely known
for its association with the
poets Samuel Taylor Coleridge
and Robert Southey

Keswick is in the lee of the
Skiddaw group, the oldest group
of rocks in the Lake District

The county of Cumbria
was created in 1974 from
the traditional counties
of Cumberland and
Westmorland

Kendal's most famous woollen cloth was Kendal Green, said to have been worn by the Kendal Bowmen

John Ruskin, the prominent
Victorian art critic, resided
in the Lake District

A single railway line, the
Windermere Branch Line,
penetrates from Kendal to
Windermere via Staveley

The Lake District is known
for being the wettest
place in England

Famous poets moved to live
or spend time in the Lake District,
becoming known collectively
as the Lake Poets

The unique cultural heritage of the Cumberland Sausage was recognised in 2011 when the pork coil-shaped snack was granted protected status

It was here that the characters
from the 2002 Danny Boyle film
28 Days Later took refuge
and managed to escape

In 1929, a new reservoir
was needed in the north west
and the Mardale Valley was
flooded, expanding the
existing Haweswater

17 million people pay visit to the Lakes annually

Whilst it is true that
Windermere is the biggest body
of water in England, it is a more
interesting fact that it holds
an incredible 300 billion
litres of water

Printed in Great Britain
by Amazon